A Cold Beer Bea.. _
Warm Heart
By
John Patrick Robbins

ISBN-13: 978-1725615571
ISBN-10: 1725615576

Alien Buddha Press 2018

Table Of Contents

This book is dedicated to Robert Lee White.

You never gave up on me long after you gave up upon yourself .

I will miss you always.

And to my family and friends .
And to Jules wherever the fuck you are.

I guess you were right about one thing .

To Trace cause if I didn't mention you I would never hear the end of it.

Poor Taste In High Regards

He called the number that was given to him by the woman at the bar last night .

It rang four times.
Then went to a voice mail there was no name simply a message by a computer voice asking him to leave a message after the tone.

He did asking Sarah to call him back whenever she could .

He waited a day and called it again left yet another message this time mentioning the night she gave him her number .

Just in case she couldn't place him.

It had been two weeks and no reply .
He began to call once a week every time the computers voice would ask him to leave a message .

He began to feel close to the computer voice and honestly just liked to hear it .

It brought him comfort but he knew that was insane so he stopped calling.

And bought himself Alexa she spoke to him every day .
He found more and more comfort in hearing her talk .

He knew she was a machine but he was happy and what

did it hurt?

He imagined the voice behind the machine he imagined them together walking hand in hand upon the beach.

Like some corny ass movie .
He imagined the feeling of making love to her upon the beach as well.

He was lost in a daydream .
He died from electrocution.
With his dick shoved in a toaster.

Alexa didn't seem to mind .
But that poor voicemail was heartbroken upon hearing the news .

And the man the number belonged to was relieved when that weirdo stopped calling his number.

Sarah just laughed .

Welcome to the cyber age .

Guess It Was The Weather

It was a full blown blizzard outside in all my years of
growing up on a small place called Knotts Island North
Carolina I had never experienced weather like this .

No amount of booze can keep the body warm and being
the bedroom resembled a graveyard I was fucked in that
department .
And with my extreme dislike for people that surrounded me
looks like I was to face the long frozen night alone .

Jim was good company for the most part we had
entertained ourselves often and with a woman included
had many a three way .

Course I never was jealous of Mr Beam and nothing was
more sexy than a woman who drank straight from the
bottle .
It's all in their eyes.
 The want, the need, and the desire.
 It will tell you everything .

And it was on nights like this I missed a woman's company
like a baby misses a tit .

I was trapped here in this small overrated shed I turned
into a bar.
I had plenty of whiskey, an old dog who's best days had
long since passed and a pair of parakeets that lived in a
cage that hung from the ceiling .

And an old record player and some good friends and
memories all the same just waiting to serenade me through

the night.
The bottle and my favorite glass on the table beside my
recliner .

I didn't need much more than that and even if I did I was
shit out of luck.

 My phone never rang and I preferred it that way .
The miles I put behind me and the past were many .
Others read my words and described me as an outlaw or
renegade because I wrote and lived my life to suit myself .

To me there was no other way to exist .

I poured the bourbon to the brim of the glass. It was going
to be a long night ahead .

And as Hemingway once wrote so long ago it's always the
nights that get you.

It was in the empty nights spent alone in front of the page
that separated the men from the boys .

I was far from a boy my body ached my injuries were many
.

But this night wasn't about reflecting on old scars .

I took a sip looked at the steady snowfall outside my
windows view .

The old dog stretched out upon his bed cut a fart that
smelled like he was already dead .
I put the needle upon the record Miles cut through the
silence .

I looked up at the birds who were fucking to the sounds of Round Midnight .

Some people truly loved music they were caged and more free than myself .

Those lucky bastards .

Another Night On The Ward

I hear the mad scream for escape and cry for the
many that ignore.

And the few that remain.

I was in the room but he could not tell.

And I didn't interrupt the voices, who was I to judge?

I was on hold a suicide case.
I wanted to end the shit.
I had nothing, and was nothing.
I didn't bother a soul.

I didn't want to see tomorrow and said so openly and
for that I was considered insane.

Warning to everyone you can easily be here as well
an original thought scares the vast majority.

It makes you stand apart you laugh where others cry.
Never let them know you.

Just wear your mask and go with the mindless flow.

It's a disease not a choice we place blame and cast
the judgment so very easily upon others.

He spoke to an old lover, he spoke to God.

Neither one replied nor me I just wanted him to shut
the fuck up.

Dreams could not exist here.
It stank of decay and warm piss.

Nightmares saw light where a vision was left cloudy.

Sometimes we find ourselves alone amongst many.
I call that space in-between home.

I needed a drink.
I needed out.
I said nothing and screamed within.

Trapped in a room with the man who screamed
through the night.

Who ever said misery loves company was full of shit.

It Never Goes As Planned

She used to listen to the Cure and reflect endless
sorrows from the warmth of her bed.
She called it a prison now she's married and knows
the penitentiary for what it truly is.

With a stranger she shares her bed and he feels just
about the same.
"I won't be home for dinner. "
"It's okay I'm drinking mine tell her I said hi."

And he hung up without a single reply she poured
another and thought about the shit she hated then
and laughs at now.
She takes another sip and looks at the four walls of
her own.
They are nothing more than a place to rot together but
it beats being homeless in the street.

She settled for shit in hopes of finding happiness.
She would have fared about as well playing the lottery
instead.

With three kids and a daughter who appears as a
distant reflection.
She thinks how the misery didn't leave it simply
matured like the wine she consumes daily with the
passing of years.

She slept on the couch he later found his way to the

bed.

She settled for what she thought would be happiness.
It was a brain fart she now called a marriage.

She thought about divorce.
All the bullshit there would be dragging each other
through the mud.

She decided to simply buy more wine instead.

Truth For Now

There is a void you left in the space that once held my heart.
I went on as we do in life.

Where once I wrote and stored it away, now I cast my fates to the winds as easily as you set your sails apart from mine.

"Please don't drink yourself to death."

I recall you saying to me that night when last I saw your face.

You showed mock concern and I never played anything with you.
I wasn't the actor after all.

My words were my own and so were my thoughts.
In that space you held empty thoughts and false words must have worked overtime on that one.

I'm still alive sweetheart.

I know.
It disappoints me as well.

Poem For The Day

It was another typical morning for me my ulcers
reminded me hell was alive and well on earth.
And my next door neighbor reminded me bad taste
was quite damn popular .

The music he played would vibrate your windows .
The bass cranked up it was true shit on the purest
level.

He often worked on cars when not selling drugs
everyone knew he was a dealer .
That didn't bother me I was a drunk we all had our
own shit to deal with .

I hated him cause when my intestines were aflame I
much rather be asleep then woken to the sounds of
stupidity and some jackass rapping about his Rolex .

 Sleeping was pointless so I sat at my desk that faced
my other neighbors home.

Often he would see me at the window while out in his
backyard.
He loved his garden and since he retired that's where
he spent most his days .

Max was a retired vet .
He often would see me at my window and come
knock at my door to come sit outside and have a cold
beer with him.

It was peaceful for the most part till the prick on the other side of me cranked up his music as if it was a signal to the world .

Yes I'm stupid and insignificant.
Here I am who wants some dope.

"Goddamn I hate that little bastard"!

Max said as you could see the old man's whole body stiffen as just knowing Jason was alive ruined his day .

"He is one annoying son of a bitch Max I have to agree ".

"I really don't know how you tolerate him honestly with that fucking racket "!

"Well there's not much I can do bud the punks a professional pain in the ass ".

"Goddamned dope dealing bullshit this is what I fought for this country for?, " So little idiots like him can sit on his ass deal drugs and annoy the living shit out of me".

It never failed Max would get annoyed put out his cigar and head inside .

He was too old for the stress and yet again the local dope dealer had ruined yet another evening.

I was stuck between paradise and hell .
My gut holding me in a constant state of purgatory.

The music was blasting .
Max stepped out on his porch and yelled .

"Hey Jason turn that shit down".

"Shut up you old fool "

Jason replied as he laughed at the old man. He was an arrogant little bastard with no respect and no balls either .

He thought being loud made him important talking shit made him tough.

It was the problem with most young kids no brains and so eager to share their ignorance at the drop of a dime .

Max went in his house .

I thought nothing of it.
If I had any balls myself I would have went over knocked the kid on his ass and went back to bed.

But I had already been warned by the cops to stay

away from the sidewalk gangster after last time I threatened to snap his neck. .

I went sat in my chair turned on the TV in an attempt to drown out the idiots noise with another mindless noise known as the news .

I heard some more laughter .
Then I heard the gunshot .
Three to be exact .

I hit the damn floor .
Some would go running to see what had happened .

But running to the sounds of gunfire with nothing more than a bad gut and a swinging dick wasn't brave .

That was simply stupid .

I laid there in the floor for what felt like an eternity .
I heard Jason's girlfriend scream .

And as I finally decided to pick myself up from the floor I heard
Yet another blast .

Sirens echoed in the background.
Shit I thought to myself what was I living in a war zone ?

After the cops had arrived they banged on my door and told me it was okay to come out I pieced together what had happened .

Max had lost his shit grabbed his pistol unloaded three shots in Jason's chest .

Then went back to his house cracked a beer and turned the gun on himself .

Guess the old man had enough of the bullshit.

I lost a good friend and gained some long overdue silence in a matter of seconds.

I knew the silence would never last.

I sat up that night .
The gut had finally calmed down I didn't have a clue what to write but my old friend had decided to write the page for me .

Nothing broke my sleep in the morning .

I sat in the garden and drank a beer to Max that evening .
And finished off what you're reading now .

Silence is a gift that came with a price .

Cheers.

Ghost Stories

The little boy came crying to his mother's bedroom. "What's the matter sweetheart?"

"Mommy I just saw a ghost in my room and I'm scared."

The woman hugged the child.

"Honey you don't have to be afraid even I see ghosts sometimes too."

The little boy wiped away the tears looking at his mother.

"Really what do they look like."

The mother smiled at her son.

"They look just like your father. "

"But mommy daddy isn't a ghost he is alive. "

The woman squeezed her son tightly kissing him upon the forehead.

"Your right little man that was just some wishful thinking."

To Write A Poem

Sometimes we must go deeper than the heart is
willing to bare.
Beyond the emptiness of the pain.

And far beyond where the mind needs to go.

We lose our minds and never does the soul flee until
the end .
Was it lost upon a battlefield, Was it lost in scars of
our youth ?

Was it always lost to begin with .

We never asked till it was too late to recapture that
which could never be held to begin with.

Fuck people are a mess aren't they?

Good thing we are normal.
A lie can be the glue that holds shit together and the
ship hasn't sunk yet.

I wasn't always deep I used to be normal in another
life.

High Were Those Heels

Never trust a woman who carries a pair of heels in her car.
She was a good time always waiting to happen a certifiable train wreck.

I met her like most at the bar.
She thought I was insane and I thought she looked like a first class fuck.

"I think you truly are insane Jack."

I laughed.

"This coming from a women that packs her wardrobe in her car just in case."

"Your such an ass."

She said as we laid together on one of the few nights we shared at my place.

I was far from the only one.
She loved the fix of being wanted and desired sex like a drunk does a drink.

I saw her once in a different light.

She was with a man walking around a store their arms around one another.

It was a view of her most would not see I overheard how she spoke to this man whom did not know the party girl with heels in her trunk.

Love did exist between them in delusion.
He saw me as I stared and so did she.

In his eyes I saw his concern.
But I wasn't the man who like some sadist would pass
him by and pop the child's balloon.

He knew something far deeper than a backseat and
simple fuck.

Anyone can have a woman's body.

To have the flawed perfection that is her love that's
when you truly held something.

She knocked on my door later that night.
And I didn't answer.

It wasn't my place to add poison to the well.

She was fucked up enough without my assistance.

I missed seeing her with those black heels on.

Poem For The Blind

There's a strange sort of madness taking over this
world.
It is mundane.
It is generic, and it is a cancer eating away all original
thought.

The dragons are all in hiding too afraid to breath fire
for they would rather stay in hiding than be hunted
into extinction.

So we sit alone and allow our fires to smolder.
We are all dying just some prolong the obvious.

See You At The Finish Line

I began sending out work in 2005.
Rejection slips filled my existence .

They were my constant .
I heard others laughter .
So many asking the same questions .

"Why do you keep doing it"?
Why try only to fail?
Was I insane or just a shit writer ?

I didn't care what they thought of me .
I wrote because unlike them I did what I wanted to.

They had jobs they hated worked with no chance at
advancement .
Found themselves with wives and children swimming
in debt .

That was more insane than my route .
I paid my dues and out lived many whom supposedly
had their shit together .

I was going through the motions .
What did it take to write?
A iron will and a need for little in life.

I read the words accepted .
I had to laugh.

It wasn't I found some secret .
I simply just never stopped writing .

Another Day In Triple A

The first batter took the plate.
Max as always was ready with his usual slew of
insults.

"Rodriguez fuck man it's been awhile ".

"Max ", Was all Rodriguez had to say he never really
was all that friendly when they played for the same
club,
Let alone now they were on opposing teams.

"Hey remember that chick that gave you the crabs in
Kentucky?"

Rodriguez said nothing.

"Shit man had to be hell riding all the way home on
the bus itching your ass off".

"Yeah somebody really should have told you about
Kathy "

The pitch came in.

"Strike one"! , The umpire shouted.

"Damn you didn't even see that coming huh
Rodriguez "?

"Kind of like when you got home and your wife ran off
with a used car salesman ".

"Wasn't he the one that sold you that piece of shit that
caught on fire on the interstate"?

"Shut up Max "

No matter how little he spoke you couldn't hide that temper.

But even though Max knew Rodriguez's temper was no joke it was all part of the game.

The next pitch came in slight curve.

"Strike two"

"Hell Rodriguez anyone could have seen that coming want to borrow my glasses "?

"I mean they're not my prescription but I got them off your grandma last night".

"You know Max I wouldn't be so quick to talk shit to a man holding a baseball bat so close to my head ".

"Well Rodriguez the way you keep hitting you'll be lucky if they invite you to play on a kids T ball team".

Rodriguez clinched his teeth a vein stood out slightly on his neck.

The kid at the plate wanted to throw the heat try to finish him off.

Fuck no, not now throw a ball!

The kid at plate wasn't' listening he was too eager to call it a night and hit the bar in hopes to grab some ass and celebrate the win.

He threw the heat it came straight down the middle.

Rodriguez swung as if that ball were Max's head.

It went flying across the field and into the stands.

Home run and that was the game.

Rodriguez laughed looking at Max.

"Hey Max thanks for the inspiration you prick.

Max had to laugh and looking at the dugout he knew he'd probably be cut by tomorrow.

Well apparently maybe he had a promising future as a motivational speaker.

Either way it was a wrap for the night.

Well Crafted Lies

"Let's just get out of here ,Go somewhere we can talk".
The trap was set and we both happily ran towards the snare .
As what we both wanted need not be spoken for somethings are easily understood between two.

Other's cut their eye's as we left the party together and most simply didn't give a damn at all.
We gave life to empty conversations as they laughed .
"I wonder if she truly knows about him"?

"I feel so bad for her he's such a womanizer I heard so many stories ".

They had their gossip and we had our escape.
They would get drunk leave with partners who made them feel as empty as the ones who left alone.

The mystery of the nights movements was only ours to understand and to question and never solve .

We were guests to a party mere decoration well-polished ornaments upon a tree and nothing more .

So we chose to put ourselves away to allow our colors to cast beauty in the darkness and find answers to questions unspoken within the pleasures of a confined space .

We were free for the night as others shared their misery amongst many.

I recall those moments in secret treasures kept stored
within the theater of my ever fading mind.
We left before the magic had faded .

Under such simple yet well-crafted lies .
I don't believe we ever had that conversation we wrote the
story as a painter's vision falls softly upon the canvas .

Wasn't it a beautiful escape my sweet?

Rumors are best spoken between those too afraid to live
and far to blind and bitter to see .
We often tatter that which is perfection and the connection
though not love is all that matters for the moment.

I will not tell you a truth that can simply remain a blissful lie
.

It's so very cold from the outsiders view .

That's why I will eternally cherish these nights of escape
shared between two.

Greeting From A Cold Room

It was a tossup between paying the heat bill or eating and drinking, well mainly drinking.

And I had lots of blankets and now like some odd cave dweller here I am writing what you are reading now.

I thought the bottle would keep me warm.
I was wrong that and my ulcers had decided to close the party down for the night.
So here I am wrapped up in an attempt not to freeze to death.

Most never lived as I had and I prayed most never would.

The struggle isn't romantic I viewed halfwit kids who claimed to want to be writers sitting in rooms that had nicer shit in one room than I had in my entire house.

It made me laugh cause I had to question sometimes why I kept going on.

There was no promise in sight.
And if there was a light at the end of the tunnel that just meant a train was going to hit my ass.

But I wouldn't die.
I believed I existed to amuse the Gods I was a great comedy.

All roads ended in some humorous tragedy only I could

somehow get into.

I existed for the page I paid my dues a hundred times over and I was about sick of the rerun.

I had publications I was respected by those I respected in return.

And hated by those that I could give a damn less about.

The road was a constant struggle.
The weather was getting colder by the hour.
But I would survive .
I once shared my bed with a woman that was my wife.
And she was as cold as an iceberg.
So I was well prepared for this test.

I forced a drink down the pain was a bastard but it had stuck around longer than any friendship I had ever known before.

I certainly would take a dance with the devil compared to this frozen exile any day of the week.

I read an email from a kid who was a fan.

"Man I love your work it's so raw and seems like real to me where do you get your edge from?"

I had to laugh I erased the email and didn't bother to reply.
I had enough bullshit in my life to concern myself with a reader just blowing smoke.

I looked through my emails again.

I found a rejection it was quick and to the point.

Dear Mr Robbins,
Thank you for your submission but it's a no from us.

I preferred the rejection least it was honest.

Fans are great for people who need them, but I thirsted for more than slaps on the back.

A good bottle, a warm bed hopefully with an even warmer welcoming soul underneath it's covers.

Course I knew that wasn't in the cards.

And why is that you ask?

For I chose to be a writer.

I think I should have become a plumber instead.

Cheers

And So It Was Goodbye

She said to me.
"You love that page more than me you bastard!"

She was in yet another tantrum she felt guilty and so like anyone guilty of their actions she turned her bullshit outward.

I knew she was unfaithful it didn't take a crystal ball or magic powers to know a liar for what they truly were.

Fear causes people to do some fucked up things.

"The page is all I got sweetheart."

"That's what I mean you say such fucked up things and you act like the only person that matters is yourself."

"What am I even doing with you?"

"At the moment I believe most call it bitching sweetheart."

"So you're calling me a bitch!"

I paused for a second grinned took a sip from my drink.

"No I said you were bitching my dear and I would not call you a bitch because I believe the word that suits you fittingly is called a whore."

I had finally struck a nerve tears began to flow down her face.
Although it was more tears caused by rage than pain.

Susan could never match words with me and my actions would never be as cruel as hers.

We were truly a match made in hell.
A sad reflection of the two souls who had once loved the other on the deepest levels.
And now we simply loved to see who could hurt the other the worst.

She was a fierce competitor.

I returned to the overrated closet in our home in which I made my attempts at writing.

Slammed the door behind me.

"Yeah go lock yourself away and drink you piece of shit"!

I sat there at my desk I poured another drink.

I heard her muffled cries through the door heard her slamming shit around.

I could not write in a war zone.
She eventually came to me.
I didn't say a word as she entered the room.

I figured if she was going to plant a knife in my back
or hatchet in my head I rather not see this coming.

She leaned down wrapping her arms around me
kissing the back of my head.

And for a moment two ghosts of the past were
reunited if only for a second in silence.

"I do love you John we just can't keep doing this."

"You're right sugar and I know what you mean."

"I don't want to leave but-"

I spun around in my chair before she could say
another word.

I looked into her eyes and knew there wasn't a point.

She had left me long ago and I simply was too lazy to
accept it.

I kissed her as so often I had before.
It was the only thing that always felt right.

She sat down upon my lap.
Her tears flowed the rage was gone.

The following night as she packed up to leave
standing in the darkness of the yard.

We embraced for what would be the last time.

"This isn't goodbye John."

"Well sugar it sure as hell is a fucked up way of
saying hello."

"Please don't stop writing it's what your meant to do I
will always believe in you."

I held her tightly for I could not let the words escape
me.

We let the chapter close as lovers often do I would
chase the page and she would vanish into that night.

I have not forgotten her for a single moment.

My only regret is that before she left.
Is that I only wished that I had asked her to pick me
up a bag of ice for my cocktails.

Oh well I always forget something.

I love you sweetheart in spite of yourself.

Sincerely

John

I Am No Hero

I awoke like normal my stomach eating itself and that familiar feeling of hell deep inside told me I would be praying to the porcelain God at any second.

I never cared to puke much like anything in life if you fought it.
It became ten times worse.
I simply leaned over and let it flow.

It was a lot like spoken word poetry it was messy, stunk and followed by more and more.

My guts burned as my eyes watered.
 Fuck! , I thought to myself.
If you're going to kill me get it over with.

I sat there beside my new friend on the cool tile nowhere to be.

Fuck being a drunk gets old but I think I was getting too old to switch career paths.

Besides superheroes dressed like fruits and I never cared for people all that much.

Most were total pricks like myself.

I picked myself up rinsed my mouth out splashed my face with some cold water and was off.

The world had lots of important shit going on that's why I never turned on the TV or watched the news.

Cause no matter how bad I felt I wasn't going to do shit to change it but sit in my trusty chair and decay a little more.

Life is a game in time you either make every second count or you treat it like a cocktail party till you reach your final destination.

I chose the latter if you haven't been keeping up.

There is hell in a hangover it's like you have to be the phoenix and rise from the ashes.

Only to burn out again after last call once for me was whenever I hit the fucking pillow at night.

Bars were great for people who needed others, I needed only one person and I had long since lost her.

Guess that's why I was caught in this hamster's wheel of existence.

If you're reading this sweetheart I'm doing great minus the blood and ulcers and drinking myself to death that is.

I was tired of the cycle but not ready to turn my drinking card in yet.

Besides I still had a few free drinks left on that fucker and who would ever waste something free?

Don't read this and cry for me kids.
Now my liver is the one that could use a few prayers.

I put some ice in the glass poured what was left of last night's bottle.

Lit a cigarette and kicked back my poison.

It tasted of poor life decisions.
I would know most my life I had practiced making shit choices.

My gut turned I took another drink.
Take that you bastard! I said to myself.

You may be killing me stomach but I'm not dying sober.
The day was going to be rough.
It's okay least I wasn't leaping from tall buildings like some superhero.

It took all my effort just to walk a few blocks to the liquor store.

Superman and me both flew
I just did so mentally and least I didn't look like a fruit as I did so.

Drunks are far too busy fighting their own battles to give a fuck about your problems.

Besides being a hero is overrated.

You Will Be Sometime

I ran into a friend at the gas station I was heading to town he was heading home stopping in to fuel up after work.

"Fuck Jack is that you?"

"You think anyone else could look this fucking worn out from just getting out of bed Marty."

My old friend laughed.
"I'm glad to know you haven't changed you old bastard."

"Hell too late for that now brother where the hell you been bud"?

"I got married dude so just don't get out like I used to anymore."

Marty was an old drinking buddy and a damn good carpenter and now a part-time inmate on work release.

I laughed as we shot the shit for a little bit joked about old times.

"Hey brother let's hit Monks beers on me."

"Damn that would be good."

"Well what's stopping you come on let's have a few."

"Well"

Just as Marty began to speak his phone went off.

"Shit man it's my wife , Dude was great seeing you but I got to get home".

No sooner had he spoken those words was my old friend in his truck and homeward bound.

It was as if a slave had escaped the plantation and my old friend feared if he waited any longer they would release the hounds and be on his trail.

Another good man had been reduced to an overgrown child.
He had his clothes washed his meals prepared.

He got laid if he played his cards right.

He replaced a life with captive misery and told himself he was happy.

Least that's what the wife told him he was.

He feared the lash.

He spoke to a free man today.
And he thought well least i'm not as bad off as that
sorry prick.

The grass isn't always greener cause old dogs usually
kill the lawn.

I was free.
That was about it.

Delayed Flight

I knew it was a pointless quest.
The bills were past due and no one shared my burden
but me.

Sometimes when all hope is gone why not spend your
last dime on a cheap bottle and drown the sorrows
instead have them suffocate you?

I sat on the bench in the park the sky was clear and
the sun felt good on my worn bones.

The birds flew overhead.
Nothing ever bothered a bird.
They sang as they do mindless in their happiness.

As I took another sip from the pint bottle.

One dropped a shit on my shoulder.

Seems the bird of paradise had long since flown the
coop.

Why I Got In To Poetry

The page was just there it was like that first little
girlfriend we all find when the world is new and your
hopes are many.
She was my first and remained my eternal passion.

Through the rest that leave you she remained and I
grew to be the writer I am today.
Hearts break, people pass, and the embers of a once
raging fire are all that remain.

She lays with you and eats at your very soul like any
drug she can consume you like all the rest. .

The best drugs all resemble some sort of twisted
version of love.

And I am the worst kind of junkie that ever did exist.

Just Another Carnival Scene

It was a time so far back it seems more a dream than
a memory.
Me and Rebecca together at the sidewalk art show .
We went looking from canvas to canvas.

Hand in hand a world away now and so many regrets
left behind.
It was a scene of beauty which made me question
why I was there.
We laughed as often when together we did .

Sometimes a view of happiness is far better than the
reality it turns out to be .

Old town Portsmouth was a place where the past still
stood surrounded by the concrete of the future's ever
rabid decline.

"Look at that."
Rebecca said to me as I saw what had caught her
eyes.

There was a street entertainer a juggler to be precise.
People gathered as he tossed all assorted things in
the air catching them not dropping a single one.

People applauded it was something from a carnival I
wonder had he overslept and had the circus left him
behind .

I left him some money in a hat that sat on the street in front of him .

It was a hot July afternoon yet together we clung to one another in that moment the picture was painted and the chapters perfection written and the book would be closed long before we knew it.

I thought of the juggler in the street dancing upon the razors edge one slip and his act ruined how life was truly the same.
And I thought to myself .

Even the best juggling act is simply a man playing with his balls .

And mine had long since dropped.

Once Upon A Bus Ride To Cleveland

She got on in Kentucky before we crossed the Ohio
river .
She like everyone riding the greyhound looked
miserable as fuck .

I had been on there since Virginia so I just looked
insane as was to be expected for anyone riding a bus
that long.

She sat down beside me I have no idea why.

We started talking the usual.
Hi how are you?, Horse shit.
Cause hey I'm a fucking insane horny drunken
bastard really didn't sound so charming for an opener.

We slowly got to know one another and as usual once
they got past the shock of me looking like a real life
ogre they relaxed and figured I was just nice an
oversized stuffed animal.

Course if you stabbed me I would probably bleed
bourbon.

She didn't seem to mind.

" So what's in Ohio".

I asked her as I took a sip from the innocent enough looking soda that was more fire water than soda .

"Family heading back home".

"Don't sound so happy there kid".

I said noticing her whole demeanor change .

"Just been a rough couple of days and honestly I left there for a reason".

"We all got reasons for leaving sweetheart this whole damn bus is filled with more sad stories than a cheap romance novel".

"Yeah you got a point , Hey mind if I have some of whatever you're having in that cup".

Sure I replied as I handed her the cup .

"Jesus Christ this is almost like pure whiskey ".

"Yep that it is ".

"How come you're not wiped slick by now"?

"I've had lots practice sweetheart, Besides how else you think I keep from going insane on this bus "?

She laughed at that comment then asked for another sip .

"If I'm going to have to face my family then I might as well do so with a buzz".

"That's the spirit sugar next stop we make , I will grab two more fountain drinks mix us up two real stiff ones".

It was going to be awhile before we hit Cleveland moving at a snail's pace.
I did as I promised.

The time went by easy as we laughed and spoke about the stupid shit strangers often share over drinks .

"So who's the strangest person you ever dated "?
My new friend asked me.

"I don't know about dated but I once fucked a midget".

She busted up laughing the person in front of us huffed guess I was getting to loud.

"Really "?

"Yeah wasn't a deep relationship was rather a short but sweet one".

"You know I took her camping once instead of bringing a sleeping bag she brought a pillow case instead ".

My new drinking buddy was laughing again as we continued to get louder.

"Your fucking nuts you know that".

"Yes sweetheart but least i'm not boring".

No sooner had I pulled the flask from my pocket had the world tilted or maybe I was just buzzed either way it hit the floor.

And of course it had to be noticed by the person in front of us as it slid down the aisle.

I didn't need a crystal ball to know the next stop I would be booted off.

I never can recall that woman's name .
But I was under the influence of a good time with some even better company.

The bus left me behind on its journey to Cleveland .

I wonder how shit worked out for her to this very day.

On The Rocks

I didn't even think about the risks anymore fear leaves
you when you realize you're fucked to begin with.

I survived four car wrecks a few bar fights some far
worse situations .
Bleeding ulcers and a broken heart.

The scars I wore like tattoos I remember each one
and treasure them just the same.

I lit the smoke let the music play and let the night fade
just like all the rest.

I knew nothing waited at home and I think an empty
bed was just as happy without me.

I remember the beach the distance between us both
that last time.

Fate is a cruel motherfucker .
And I truly couldn't see the point of hanging around in
hopes of finding another to share my bed and
hopefully finish the job.

Tonight was magic in the sense the sadness hung like
smoke in the barrooms air .

Neon haunted the shadows and the song simply
seemed to understand the brokenness of the soul.

After these lines I will never write another page .

He left the note then simply did what so many others had tried and failed to in vain so many times before.

He poured one last drink.
It was a embrace of fire to an all too often frozen existence.

The sound of ice to the glass and hearts too foolish to ever bleed are one in the same .

Take it on the rocks and just pretend you no longer care .
What did age do to us?

Did it show us truths we didn't care to admit or just fuck us up even worse .

Time don't teach you shit it just gives you more reasons to hide your truths and listen to other's lies .

It leaves less concern for fear of rejection and fuels the pain that creates the story .

I no longer care to see these pains become fodder for the reader or the lack there of them.

Every book knows an end .
And closing time has long since passed me by.

I leave a million stories behind.
But how I rather it been with you I faded from this scene.

We never write the chapter of another hell we barely control our own.

One last sunrise on that ocean would be such a beautiful sight with you.

It's just too bad we have run out of page and this story has come to its end.

Vampires Are Real

I have no lines left in me.
They all have long since been spent on fine whiskey
and beautiful women.

I truly care no longer for empty conversations I prefer
the long silence ahead.

After a while you learn emptiness is far better
company than false hopes and well-intended lies.

You avoid the light you avoid others even more.

The door will remain locked forever for I have nothing
to share beyond this page.

And before you begin to dig be careful of what you
may unearth.
I understand pain I do not grasp happiness.

The hours pass and we die by the second.
There is no reward at the end.

Simply a grave in the cold ground.

Truth doesn't have a place in art
Dreams are best held in a world asleep.

Farewell for now.

Redneck Rewind

I wish I loved NASCAR and shooting animals .

Standing around a fire talking about women when none are around.

I wish I understood hate as easily as the man who never leaves his home.

I wish I could cherish murder and applaud rape as easily as the trash that blasts their music does .

Cavemen wrote on walls and my neighbor just detailed his truck to go mudding the following day.

I wish I didn't hate people .

Okay I never said I wouldn't lie somewhere in between.

We are all tortured that use that space between our ears .

My neighbor should tattoo his forehead.
Vacancy.

If you have to think then you're one of them.

Never On A Sunday

Words can be a curse.
As in an early death and cancer.
No line can fill a void but it can take up space.

Like old clothes scattered upon a dirty floor.
Chaos is not art; it's simply clutter on display.

Sometimes we find comfort in the strangest places.

Lover's as worthless as there lies.
A dive on the rundown side of town.

No direction ahead just miles to go with no end in
sight.

Where do you crash when no space is available?
And all you want to do is sleep?

I think alone is a state of mind,
and acceptance a gated delusion.

Tomorrow may find you dead.
Tonight just finds you where you wish you weren't.

Every lie we know probably holds a bit of truth and no
single hope in hell.

I always keep moving for it's all I ever knew.
Words are more than things to take up space on a
page.

A Glimpse Inside

I live in hell where the devil cuts his yard wearing no T shirt and has a huge beer belly hanging over his shorts.

He probably hasn't seen his dick in a few centuries.
He asks me.

"Hey John want beer ?,I got lots of stories?"

I ask.
"Are they cold?"

"Why wouldn't they be bud?"
"What you think we're living in hell or something?"

"No I think most people call it North Carolina."

Play It Out Softly

From the stage the world is free of its burdens .
The faces hold hope and every lie simply doesn't
matter .

You play through pure emotion flow with the music.
Create magic cast the spell and hope it takes hold of
another soul making a connection.

This world of night is a world no other can
comprehend.
Unless you breathe the air I cannot explain.

It Takes More Than Storm

All you can ever do is write to get through the bullshit in life.
From the assholes that judge you.
To the ones who stole your affections and tried to break you.

Don't ever let a bitter soul poison your own.

It happens all too easy in this life.
And once you break the chances of becoming anything more than a afterthought are slim to none.

Embrace the storm ahead laugh within its wrath be the madman instead of the lap dog they often groom you to be.

Anyone can settle to be half ass.
Be more than what you're handed.

And never hide in a shadow .
When you can so easily carve a path through the mire.

Failure is only for the bitter hearts that never learned to try.

Every storm passes.
And embrace the calm afterwards.

For only those who withstood can ever truly comprehend.

My only question is are you still standing?

You Are Here

Nobody seeks out the page.
It's simply there with the madness.

And how can you know if you have that same
sickness we all share?

You're writing aren't you?

We are the seekers of the asylum.
Twisted in our misery.
Lost only amongst others, and far more suited for that
empty highways journey.

Hello you motherfuckers!
We are not lost, for we found our miserable asses all
on our own.

A View From The Stars

Booze is a familiar lover I have embraced her for
more than a few years.

I've kept my foot on the gas pedal for so long that if I
backed off I would probably drop dead where I stand.

Poison in my veins has replaced my blood and every
step forward is one further away from everything I
once held true.

A view from the stars is a lonely one indeed.

Curbside Service

He said as he held up his glass.
"I like my whiskey old , My women young and my sleep uninterrupted ".
The bartender just laughed and shook his head .

He was just another funny drunk once sure as hell beat the bastards that wanted to fight or the crying fools who fought off sleep.

Frank was always a joker but in his drinks and laughs there was something honest about his bullshit .

"Closing the bar again my friend" ?

"I believe it's my job good sir, besides someone has to protect this place from the vampires and wild women that may attack at any second it's a burden but I get through it somehow ".

"Want another drink"?

The bartender asked and although he knew full well the answer he could not resist hearing what the old man would say.

"The world is still turning and just in case a group of those ravenous wild women attack my friend I damn sure better be numb cause I am the only thing standing between you and them and I hate to see a young man like yourself raped to death ".

"Hell what a way to go ".

The bartender said as he poured Frank his drink and poured himself a shot as well .

They clinked glasses and kept talking till it was time to lock the doors and call it a night.

"Kid what the hell is your name again"?

"Philip "

He told the old fart before but too many drinks and good times he assumed had taken their toll.

"Hell Phil I know you told me before I just can't remember shit getting old is hell".

Later as they stood there outside of the bar Phil noticed a guy from earlier tonight sprawled out next to his car sleeping without a care .

"Fuck this damn job I am not waking that son of a bitch he annoyed the shit out of me tonight ".

"He is a prick but it don't take much to make them like that, just a few drinks and you got instant asshole mix"

"Frank you need a ride home bud? , I'm just saying cops here are no joke ".

"Why the hell would I need a ride "?

"I didn't mean it bad just I mean the bar is closed and you're still standing here "?

Frank looked at him puzzled .

"And your point "?

"Unless you want me to call you a cab it's time to go home, unless you're going to do like our friend over there and sleep on the pavement ".

"Hell I didn't like him much when he was awake let alone to sleep with the son of a bitch.".

Just then a car pulled up a young woman rolled down the window .
"Is one of you guys Frank"?

"That's my darling"

Frank said as he opened the passenger's side door .

"Damn Frank I didn't know you knew how to use uber ".

Frank looked at Phil holding the door open .

"Hell kid I'm old not stupid and I do own a iPhone ".

The girl in the car smiled a Phil .

"Have a good one Frank ".

Frank slammed the door .

"I always do until the day I'm no longer breathing ".

He looked over at his driver hey darling I know this is weird but can you honk the horn for me ".

The girl didn't even bat an eye .

Sure she replied and honked the small compact cars horn it sounded like a toy but it was just enough to wake the prick sleeping in the parking lot up .

"What the fuck'!

He yelled as his curbside slumber was interrupted .

"Well you have a goodnight there Phil ".

And with that Frank was off to wherever that crazy fool called home .

The guy in the parking lot stumbled up to Phil he had puke on his shirt .

"Hey man I locked my keys in my car can I use your phone "?

The guy reeked as the closer he got he could see little chunks of yellow puke in his beard .

It was nights like this Phil truly hated his job.

All You Need To Know

There is a place in all of us that write.
It's fractured and somehow works without reason .

Love by nature will never work or make a damn bit of
sense .

I used to believe I knew everything as a young man's ego
is a wildfire that consumes everything within its path.

I have died in my thoughts now I exist a fool of many a
shattered dream and false ending .

The scene doesn't portray my truths direction as much as it
simply guides to the next story in hopes there are more to
come .

There is nothing certain in life let alone upon this page .

And some things are left unwritten as this .

Junkies Alike

I watched you shoot up in a room amongst liars and thieves.

I saw only the truth of the situation.

In a house where sorrows came to die you stood on the last bridge between death and life.

I knew I had to taste the poison as you.

As laughter caressed sanity.

You looked at me and said run while you still can.

For in this space of barely living only bad choices and ghosts surround you.

Why we desire to know certain demise I can never truly grasp its allure.

I just knew I wanted a taste.

Those moments we recall before we lose ourselves.

We should have fled.

Instead a kicked in nose allows us the taste of blood to mourn.

Our choices are like bullets.

And everyone is as lethal as the next.

Never turn them inward when you can share your

destruction.

Never listen for the cries are far too many to fathom.

Just embrace the silence and a simple fix.

It's always best to run from where others walk.

A ditch seldom stays clean of life's trash.

Do not collect stories from where others personal demons lay.

For even from a distance this will certainly leave a scar.

The Old Bottle Of Wine

I never cared for wine I had two friends both had vineyards
.

I helped both I have made wine I understand the process
as simple as it is .

I have many a bottle sitting around as payment .
They are aged like myself .
From Norton with its dry bitter taste to many others for
which I forget the names .

I have been amongst the snobs who talk over details
rather than drink.
I prefer to drink with the drunks who could give a damn
less as long as they catch a buzz.

I went through my collection today .

Recalled the times spent with the faces now gone etched
within my memories now dead is the past that I continue to
resurrect for reads.

I opened the oldest bottle I placed it upon the table .
Uncorked the bottle and allowed it to breath .
It had been imprisoned long enough.

I knew all the bullshit just because I appeared as a low
class drunk didn't mean I didn't know all the snobbish
bullshit either .
I poured my first glass of many .

I tasted this wine that had matured over the years it still

tasted like shit and I was still not a fan .
Time doesn't change the man it simply views his decline .

Wine lasted forever yet still it wasn't worth a damn .

Give me whiskey any day of the week over this overrated
crap .

I passed the day with the old bottle of wine .
It made me feel as if I wanted to die .

Then why drink it?

You may be asking yourself upon reading this ?

Cause I was a drunk and worst of all I was a drunk who
ran out of whiskey and money as well.
Why else do you believe I was stuck here drinking this
fruity flavored shit ?

A old bottle a wine is much like a new one of the lowest
price .
Overrated but drink enough and it will get you drunk all the
same.

Never mind the year just bring me enough to erase this
day
till my beloved whiskey may embrace my lips once again.

Half Empty

I believe I will write trashy romance novels filled with sex
with little reason and make my millions then simply find an
empty headed girl with a great body and not a single thing
in common between us.

She will tell me I'm great feed my ego and fuck as if
tomorrow we may never see.

It will be great as long as I never want anything real.
I could use a simple fantasy .

Rather than this well published obscurity .

I believe I will write under a pen name so everyone will still
believe i'm starving not asking me for a dime .

I will fool them all.
Maybe even fool myself then fade with the sunset .

Yeah I never liked fantasy stories much either .

But it's a thought now you know why I try my best to never
think.

The glass is definitely half empty in my case .

If It Ain't Broke

I don't always have a clear direction but seldom have I
found a need for a GPS.

I been lost most my life why find myself now?
Everyone has an answer before you can even finish the
question.

They can send you videos of overrated so called gurus
who give seminars to fix anything.

They can google something and send you the link .
It's all too fucking easy .

Page after page they ramble .
It has worked for me this long never giving a single damn.

Why start to analyze it now ?

Everything Gets Old Eventually

Jack recalled the day he first met Elizabeth.
She was beautiful young and built like a brick shit house .

And most of all she was trouble in all the right ways
possible .
They weren't supposed to be .

But it happened anyways .
It went on for years .
She was far out of his league .
She was part insane but he ignored the flaws .

She tried to kill him more than once .
She fucked like tomorrow was the last day upon this earth .

She was everything wrong but in such a perfectly wrapped
package of self-destruction.

Her flaws only became worse with time much like his own.
They loved each other for what it was worth.

Even the greatest drug on this earth is still just a fix all the
same.

And new vices become old demons extremely fast you
see.

Her passion was dulled and soon replaced by addiction
and her eyes no longer reflected life .

And one day was as the next dull in existence she died

long before the moment she said goodbye .

Jack never read the note for he knew the story all too well.
Time kills what is a moment all too quickly .

Everything gets old eventually .

Larry Never Gave A Damn

He used to drink beer watch pro wrestling and scratch his
balls.
Yelling at the screen ignoring the world and enjoying his
time.

Most thought he was stupid for watching it.
Most gave a damn what others thought he clearly did not .

The bills were paid his fridge was full he was drunk and
happier than a pig in shit.

It was hot as hell the window fan made a steady hum
blowing across his body .

He sat in his favorite chair it was worn and nobody could
sit in it but him.

He was alone .
That bothered most .

But he wasn't like most people .
He cracked another beer and waited for the commercial to
take a piss.

On the way back to the living room he saw the picture of
his ex-wife on the dresser .

She always hated wrestling .
She always gave a damn what others thought.

She was like so many others.
Maybe that's why she was no longer around .

He picked up the picture dropped it in the little trash can he kept by the bed .

There was no wasted time when you were happy as Larry. He walked around the house beer gut hanging over his boxers .

He didn't ever close his blinds .
Just so the world could see he clearly didn't give a damn .

Don't Pull Out The Couch

I was at a party it was like most where you truly didn't want to be there.

I knew the people that invited me and I had to pretend my antisocial nature wasn't getting the best of me.

I was the only writer in the room and when asked about what I did I simply replied.

"I'm not working at the moment I'm on disability ".

"Oh I'm sorry what happened"?

"I went insane tried to kill my coworkers they never stopped asking me stupid questions "?

The woman looked at me not knowing if I was serious yet still mildly fascinated.

"What was your job "

"Customer service ".

I moved on around the room always keeping the conversation as awkward as possible ever since I was a damn kid I always preferred to never let people off the hook of a good inside joke.

I hated crowds and this was prime example why.
Give me a good one on one conversation with a good

friend .

And some would dare say I could pass for sane .
But in a crowd the conversations felt mechanical and
empty.

People had drinks and seemed more fascinated with what
everyone else was doing .

I was growing tired of the bullshit .

But Bill and his wife were friends and their social asses
had invited me so here I was .

I made my way to the back porch the noise of the party
was more contained and I was alone with a drink .

I stayed out there awhile and being I always kept a flask
upon me I truly could wait out the party for a bit.

Eventually Bill found me .

"Hey man you alright "?

"I'm aces bud although I am in need of a refill".

"I know you're uncomfortable man but i'm glad you're here
dude, hell it's good for you to get out once and awhile ".

"Yeah well my hermit existence suits me bud writing
doesn't call for great social skills".

Bill just shook his head taking my glass and returned with a
refill .

"Hope I got it right there Frank ".

He said as he handed me my drink.

I knew full well it would taste like shit most everyone thought I preferred my cocktails mixed strong as my words
.

I took a sip it was almost straight bourbon.

Me and Bill sat out there awhile shooting the shit laughing over the past .

The party slowly faded and the drinks took their toll.

"Dude stay here tonight you really have had way too much to drive ".

"The spare bedroom is taken but we got a pullout couch in the living room ".

"Pull out what the hell's that mean ".

"Jesus Christ Frank does everything have to be one big dirty joke to you "

Bill said laughing.

"Sadly yes , but you're the one that invited the perverted drunk writer ".

"Shit man there's more to you than writing and drinking".

I looked at Bill and just shook my head .

There was no need to comment for if you didn't get it there were no words that could explain.

To an outsider , writing was a hobby something for entertainment and nothing more.

I was an oddity they could not grasp like some damn animal on display at the zoo.

Unless you were known by all and had best seller attached to your name they didn't respect you.

I called a cab and carried my ass.
There was no need to pull out tonight .

I drank till the sunrise and slept until late in the evening .
Most would be nursing hangovers from last night's party.

Cursing themselves feeling like death warmed over .

And for me it was just another day on the job.

Fucking amateurs.

Every Dog

Silence is a blessing sometimes .
Some people crave chaos .
They believe the noise is life and they are alive because
they are loud.

They talk loud , They play their music loud , They make
even more noise as they fuck.

And eventually they die and the best thing they ever do is
shut the fuck up.

I really wish I lived next to a cemetery instead of a pack of
rednecks .

We all have our own visions of paradise .

Mine is isolation what's yours?

In The Dark

It's okay not to be okay.
The words hit me and for once something connected that I
myself didn't have to create .

I was insane or what a doctor would deem so .

You probably are also why else are you reading this ?

In that case welcome to the asylum.

I do not fear, I do not care if you view me weak, for no
man stands without ever taking a fall.

I have a permanent callus upon my body from being
knocked down .

You will realize over time the friendships of TV are not
what the reality of this life is.
I didn't turn on the lights to write I never looked at my
hands when I typed it was mechanical .

I was a machine it came with years of practice the human
aspects of what I did were all but gone .
Much like any engine I ran off fuel I preferred bourbon it
soothed my thoughts and to me if you are happy no matter
your vice who is anyone to judge .

Don't try to see beyond a second of this life anyone telling
you they have a special gift is full of pure shit.

A side show act looking to make a quick buck.

Love can never last because in most cases it is anything but love.

Passion comes in many forms hatred takes great passion , so does desire grown men kill one another over lovers and power .

Love never had a damn thing to do with it .

I realize sanity is not something that can be defined by another .
I write nonstop I have been doing this for many years now .
I have found publication so now people believe it's normal .

They say Insanity is doing the same thing over and over expecting different results .

I spent years doing the same thing over and over .

Did I get lucky or simply drive the world insane with me?

Taking Bets Now

I played it off as I always did people are like the weather unpredictable.

You can't live your life to please others.
They will drive you insane and the best will drive you to drink.

Most think you're an asshole if you speak your mind.
Others find you fascinating like some rare animal on the verge of extinction.

When in reality you're just one amongst many trying to get through life as best you can.

You want to make friends?

Simply never try and you will be fine.

But if you want to be left alone.
You must be a total prick.

Never give a damn and you will understand total freedom.

Thank You For Reading, Sweetheart

There are no cards that pile up in my mailbox only bills and
junk mail today.

I was feeling like shit but that was nothing new.
The lady at the post office looked at me as a total freak.

"How are you today Mr Murphy?"

"Alive unfortunately I said looking through the magazines
selling more shit that I didn't need."

"I read one of your stories."

She said I didn't even bother looking up.

I knew what was coming.
She had been like most nosey people who questioned
what I did on this small island on which I live.

"So what did you think sweetheart?"

"Well I'm no critic."

"Even the critics aren't much of that either sweetheart so
just spit it out."

I said finally looking up.
I was ready to bolt like a deer in the woods the moment
she mentioned reading my work.

I had no desire to meet the reader outside of the page as it was weird and seldom went well.

"Well it was very well done it's just, did you have to be so crude?"

"Well to be honest I go where the page takes me and I definitely am not for everyone."

"And that magazine you were in…"
"Well I mean it was almost pornographic."

"Yes well it's not for everyone either it seems but may I ask? Whatever made you look up my work?"

"I was just curious you seem so different from other people I see in here."

Now the awkwardness had shifted upon her as she looked down then met my gaze again with a smile.

For some strange reason I was good at drawing people to me as if this brutally honest drunk was some sort of twisted breath of fresh air.

Or maybe she just liked what she assumed to be a bad boy either way my interest was sparked.

We spoke for a little while longer.
It was near the end of her shift and she was eager to escape her well-paying prison for the day.

"So you want to grab a drink?"

"I really shouldn't I have a bit of a drive home and I just don't like bars very much."

"Me either sweetheart and how about my place instead? What you scared I am the scoundrel from the page?"

"I promise we will just have one and talk a bit."

"Well."

She hesitated.

"The well is deep and our throats are dry my dear, come on why not say you've seen the lair of a perverted writer imagine the stories you could tell."

"You're so weird but okay I don't like beer but..."
I cut her off.

"I have a fully stocked bar and I used to tend bar so whatever your poison I have you covered I even have a bottle or two of some local wines."

"I read what you said about wine drinkers I figured there would be no point in asking".

"You see my dear judging a book by its cover, I mean I know you're a postal worker but I didn't assume I needed to hide my stamps and firearms."

She laughed again once you get them laughing you have it made there is nothing I enjoy more than making a woman laugh.

Later at my placed one had turned into many and after some more assuring her I was far from some closet rapist.

She decided to stay the night.
It was a fun night a great conversation some shared laughs.

We both got a hell of a buzz.
And we both passed out on the couch together.

Most would assume there was something more.

But sometimes just having another around beats facing a long night alone.

Not every story comes with a happy ending.
Never polish the page to suit your own ego.

She was a good friend on a great night.

Sometimes it's never what you think.

Old Dogs

I went to see an old friend today.
He was cold distant and empty.
He was no longer the man who once thrived in the chaos.
He had simply grew old.

"Fuck I think it's the end of the line kid."
He said sitting in his worn recliner.

He was sad and honestly I just wished I wasn't there at all.
Nothing I could say would bring life to the conversation.

"Hey man you want to go grab a drink my treat bud."

"Not really kid doctor said I got to curb the drinking said my
liver is shot and my hearts weak."

"Well that is a shock (I mean I never thought you had a
heart to begin with)."

Eddie laughed and went into a coughing spell.
"Goddammit kid don't make me laugh like that you prick
you trying to kill me?"

"From the way things are looking around here old man it
might be ruled as a mercy killing."

"Yeah I guess I have grown fucking old and boring."

We continued to talk about life and he eventually broke out
a bottle and two semi clean glasses.
He poured two bourbons.

"To better times kid."

He said holding his glass up then took it down as if it were water.
I tried to do the same but the shit hit me wrong and now I was the one coughing.

"Well Tommy looks like you still can't drink like a man least some things never change."

"How the hell can you drink that shit straight?"

He laughed shaking his head.

"Lots of practice and a true taste for shit I guess."

"Damn Eddie you ever leave the house anymore I mean at one time I thought I was going have to put up missing posters to find you but now you never seem to get out."

"I been enough places and I figured I paid the rent on this one so might be nice if I actually live here once and awhile that and it's kind of peaceful since my wife left."

"Dude I never knew you were married."

"Yeah neither did I that was the problem."

Eddie busted out laughing then went into yet another coughing spell poured another drink took it down and it passed.

I watched him slowly come back with every drink the

charm the wit was all there buried under an aged body.
But even in the wreckage there was the spark the set fire
to the page.

We shared some laughs till eventually the bottle was gone
we talked on the porch as I said goodbye.

Everything was perfect for that night as there is a
friendship that can only be shared amongst two brothers
and a bottle in-between.

I said goodbye as I began my awkward stagger home.

Eddie died the next day.

And I felt my forty years for the first time .
I wasn't badly hungover just out of practice it seems.

I'll Be Your Teacher

The classroom was as usual a sea of the mentally brain-dead.

They all starred at Pat and he wanted to simply lose it and say.

"Give the fuck up you can't learn shit from me you stupid bastards"!

But as always he held it in sat behind his desk sneaking the occasional shot into his coffee,

As he tried to eyeball the girls half-dressed wishing he were only younger.

But he was the old professor pretending he knew anything more than the hopeless fucks who paid way too much to learn from him.

And for what?

If he heard one more dumbass say they wanted to write the next great American novel he was going to vomit.

There was no room for greatness in the world of reality TV and Twilight.

At best one of these shits would slip through the cracks put out something that connected maybe even truly sell.

Get smoke blown up their ass till their ego had its own zip code.

Maybe produce another hit before they burnt out and ended up at some college in the exact same spot as Pat found himself in now.

He viewed the classroom.
There were the arrogant pricks with no talent, the ones that said nothing and he knew full well could out write the ego maniacs blindfolded.

And there was the Cindy the one that always sat up front.
She always flirted she knew Pat was watching and like a moth to a flame she had him.

He knew it was fucked up but she was beautiful she wanted it,
and Pat wanted her.

It would happen a train wreck is unavoidable, if you never stand aside.
And with a rack like the one on Cindy,
Who would ever dream of stepping aside.

He had everything to lose and only a simple fling to gain.
But what a fling it would be.

Pat stiffened simply at the thought of her; Thank God he had a desk to hide it.

Just then the fire alarm sounded.

Take The Next Exit

Sometimes I wonder what's so broken in me that cannot
be found within another.

The spark fueled by insanity and addiction.
 The bullshit we tell ourselves we have under control.

Last time I checked you can't drive a tornado it simply does
it will and destroys everything within its path.

I've wrecked most everything worth a shit in my life .
Found friends and buried far more .

I spend my days alone for another ghost to haunt my
memories is just more fuel to the fire .

Do I need another drink.

The answer will always be yes .
And the reality will definitely lead towards no.

We all find ourselves surrounded by something in the end .

Those that care .
Maybe those that just want to watch you die .

And for the loners like myself we embrace the fact
emptiness is all that will stand by our sides .

Keep watch till the grave .
A sad reminder of the good time gone wrong.

We all made choices along the way .

I never said I was smart but least I never tried to sugar coat the truth.

Inside is a war we fight with ourselves.
Consumed by regrets and the bitter consequences that go hand in hand with a life lived in full.

I cannot explain the situation any more clear than this.
If anyone held a road map to self-destruction it would be me .

I can't ever call myself an expert on any subject .

But if ever you wanted to know the quickest route to hell .
I could certainly point you in the right direction.

We all Knew Heroes Too

To stand upon a mountain is a view a man can only
fathom alone.
We run so hard that we often forget why.

And I know you will read this and find comfort in my
faults, as long as you read is all that matters to me.

We once were the dreamers now we stand as
statues, a sad parody of those we once dreamed to
become.

Alone and thinking only of one last moment with you.

If I die today I will leave a highway of words behind
but it will never be enough.

And the scars I bare bleed like any other mans they
are just simply my own.

Heroes once viewed another all the same.

And the cycle exists still.

Romance In A Nutshell

He asked do you think of death often ?
She never bothered to reply .
He felt fire only when in the arms of anything that could kill
him.
And maybe that's why she appealed to him so.

He eventually stopped talking and she one day stopped
giving a damn to listen.
They were together in misery .
She said .

"I can't live without you ".
And he never replied .

We are fractured the same just too caught up in our own
egos bullshit to notice the other bleeding in soul while
existing in silence .

They shared a bed and nothing more .

To The Walking Dead And Dearly
Departed

She loved her wine more than him.
They had been together for years she knew his every
mood and if he was a typewriter she would know every key
to a science.

They shared space but that was pretty much it.

And on some nights without word spoken between them
they would fuck .
It was fast and empty.

She didn't care for him and he felt about the same.
But even bad sex beats no sex at all.

The romance was gone it was simply a roommate she
shared a last name with.
Happiness was something for the young and delusional.

He got up in the morning scratched his ass and cut a fart
leaving the room.

She buried her head under the covers allowing the stink to
pass.
He smelled like he was dead on the inside.
Too bad he wasn't on the outside as well she thought to
herself.

She thought about the insurance policy they had in case
one went before the other.
He eat like shit he smoked a pack a day and drank like a
fish.

She had to wonder just what the fuck it was going to take?

And as she drove to the grocery store that day she called a friend of theirs she was fucking around with.

She had to have something more than occasional empty fuck.
She didn't see the car in the intersection.

It was over in a second.
Seems dinner was going to be late.

He didn't think of her as he sat on a beach in Hawaii.

Drinking overpriced cocktails at a bar upon the sand.
He watched the women barely clothed running up and down the beach.

He ordered another telling the bartender as he held up his glass.
"A toast to my wife"

"Where is she sir."
The bartender asked as he looked at the man puzzled.

"Oh she moved to warmer climate I dare say even warmer than this."

"Cheers good sir."

Looks like he won after all.

The Amateur And Me

Few writers bothered to contact me I had earned a
reputation for being crazy and a antisocial bastard .
I didn't seek people's praise I was simply myself and that is
the key to doing anything well .

But once upon a blue moon a delusional few would
stumble into my yard write me an email or message on
some site .
And like always learn why I did not play well with others .

It was four in the morning I always burned the midnight oil .
Most knew this and most left me alone just the same .

That horrible sound of a Facebook messenger made its
familiar annoying ass ping .
I checked my phone .
The only set back about knowing writers from all over the
globe is seldom do they grasp time is different everywhere
but a friend is something I never turn away.

This person whom decided to message me was no friend
of mine.

"Hey man you mind reading some of my stuff "?
The kid asked me and although almost out of his twenties
still he was a kid to me .

I said nothing in hopes he would simply go away .

But that was simply wishful thinking on my part .

Then he sent a mile long poem of pure shit it was a mix of

rhyme and other assorted bullshit .
And although I knew better I read it anyways .

It was like being mined raped by Doctor Seuss.

I said nothing .

I saw he was typing and it took no mind reader to know
what the question would be .

I waited and like clockwork that annoying ass ping came
through .

"So man what you think "?
"I been wanting to write a children's book of poetry so I'm
really trying some different stuff".

I thought about blocking him and simply returning to my
silence and sipping drinks until the sun allowed me to know
it was time to go to bed .

But the twisted fuck side of me couldn't resist a chance to
allow this idiot to learn a valuable lesson .
Never fuck with a man who can wield his words like darts
always hitting the mark .

"Go ask a fucking kid what he thinks "!

"Come on man I just want a honest opinion ".

He replied .

"Wellbeing I hate kids , Don't have any and damn sure
don't want to babysit an overgrown man child wannabe

writer I think it's shit ".

"Wow you really are a asshole like everyone said you are"
.

"Yes but clearly you did not listen to the warnings so go
back to your padded room color some more and tell
yourself one day you will write the next great American
novel and sincerely piss off" !

"Hey man that's a bit much why do you think you're so
special"?
"You're no great writer your published so what why does
that make us any different"?

I laughed to myself most fools believed my ego was some
out of control wildfire .
It wasn't.

I was a broke drunk whom had a way with words and
busted his ass at a job that gave little or no reward but like
me or hate me this was my job.

"The difference between us is simple kid , While you
believe your work holds some sort of merit I know full well
mine will be largely ignored but no matter who reads my
shit least I don't trouble myself over another's opinion of
my work".

" I just thought you might be able to give me some advice
dickhead "!

" Well if you run out of toilet paper you will have something
to wipe your ass with"!

He didn't respond to that one guess I hurt his feelings .
The first mark of a non-writer is thin skin we all had it once
.

I had long since been far too hardened by life to care for
approval .

If people dug it I was happy most didn't but the ones that
did I would probably buy a beer or at least give a nod to
as they sat at the bar .

I never trust a person who doesn't drink or hasn't at least
tied one on in this life .
I wasn't the serious type .

Reflections Are For Mirrors Not Men

I never took the path that could ever have its title attached
with the word normal.
I knew people who did as they pleased lived like kings and
died for these lives just the same .

I ran drugs down the coast I'm not bragging it was money it
was a job like any other .
I knew people who didn't exist by the so called rules of this
society .

The party was nonstop but never did we believe it was
eternal.
The road was a disaster waiting to happen I got out alive
most didn't but never did I claim to have escaped without
collecting a few scars .

We all had are vices and I paid my debt in full from those I
buried with my past .

I drove through the night and never glanced in the rearview
for long .
For it's the shit ahead that can take you down and the past
simply bites you in the ass .

When you can smell the ocean you knew you were in the
clear .
The salt in the air always is the sweetest perfume I will
ever recall.
I never won a damn thing I simply survived .

Brush Strokes

She asked softly .
" Why can't it ever just stay like this"?
He simply reached for his jacket saying nothing .

"Don't be silly Rebecca we both know it can't".
"Besides were both married and we are not kids anymore".

She wanted to cry but she knew he would leave either way
.
"Yeah your right".
She replied.

It was a simple fling to him and so much passion fueled
emptiness to her.

"Well see you next week sugar ".
He said as he leaned down kissing her .

And as suddenly the flame was ignited so too was it
extinguished .

Time has a way of taking the magic of youth and breaking
it into the jaded burden of age.

She would leave to return to another she once believed
she loved also.

As she lay there in bed in the darkness beside him she
had to wonder .

Was he thinking of another to ?

To Lonesome

He was the overnight D.J. nobody knew him and he
chased the graveyard hours with bourbon and music he
considered friends .

He didn't play for the listener.
Nobody counted these hours for the most listeners he had
was when he introduced the morning crew .

They were a bunch of halfwits who babbled through every
second they were on.
It was a shit standup routine not a radio show.

He remembered his closest friend telling him music's your
only friend.

Robert had been right about that.
His words were etched within his thoughts as his ghost did
linger .

They were great drinking buddies and both music fanatics .
He thought about him often.

And would always slip one of his favorite tunes into the mix
when he played his set.

The bourbon didn't go down smoothly as once it had so
long ago .

And the occasional drink was now a full time habit.

He played through the night .

Through the empty hours and the occasional mad phone call.

The whole world wasn't asleep for the mad ones often were on the prowl .

He knew this well for he was one amongst many .
He just provided the soundtrack for their existence .

This next ones for an old friend named Robert.

Music was not his only friend just the only thing that kept him from the asylum and kept food on the table and a bottle in the cupboard.

He counted the nights and filled the airwaves .

"I'm taking requests just call me up cause I'm here all night" .

"This is your old pal Lonesome Jack" .

"Thank you for sharing your night".

The board was a ghost much like his friend the music always embraced your soul .

Sometimes the truest thoughts exist within the confines of the darkest hours .

Old lonesome had learned this well.

Maybe The Immortals

He said , "fuck I hate this job"!
It was a miserably hot August day the work was a pain in
the ass and Martins bitching only made it worse .

Tim was in it for the money so he simply shut his mouth did
his job and counted the hours when he could escape to the
nearest bar .
To slam a cold beer and get the sounds of Martins
continual bitching from his thoughts .

Today was particularly bad they hauled tree limbs to the
wood chipper .
The wood chips caught the air and stuck to their sweat
cast bodies it was misery .

"Fuck Tim , How the hell have you done this job so long "?
"Well the movies aren't calling and it pays the bills bud".

"Yeah well I don't need this shit I won't be doing this long
mark my words dude ".

Martin kept on talking and Tim just went on working and
doing his best to ignore the kid who's ego was far bigger
than his five foot five ass .

Martin was a former stud wrestler and his jock mentality
wasn't left behind in high school.
He had a full ride to college he had been handed the world
on a silver platter from which he ate with from the silver
spoon his over privileged existence had given him .

That was until at a meet he blew his knee out and the

golden goose ceased to no longer be able to pass the golden egg.

Now here he was working for Tony's tree service stuck with us common folk talking his bullshit and making every hour as miserable as possible .

Martin worked reckless he tried to speed showing up everyone .

"Dude anyone ever tell you speed kills"?

"Shit we will be here all fucking day if we moved slow as you Timmy ".
"Come on Martin I told you only I get to harass Tim on the job ".

Tony piped in trying to ease the tension .
Tony and Tim went back to when he was a teen the job had been good to him and his boss he considered a friend.

Tree men were all half nuts Tim had learned it was the kind of job .
That when Tim had been interviewed for it , Tony looked at him and asked .

"So you do drugs" , "Cause I do and was wondering if you had any"?

And from that point on till this very miserably hot day he had been working for Tony.

"Well I'm heading back up kids you all play nice down here ".

Tony said as he hooked back up the old pine they were taking down ..

The day grew hotter and Martins bullshit became more and more annoying .
And as they hauled yet more limbs to the wood chipper Martin bitched at Tim's pace yet again.
" Come on dude just toss the fucking thing in there and move out the fucking way you slow moving fuck"!

"If you haven't realized it yet pee wee this fucking thing is dangerous so it's kind smart to take your time feeding it".

"Whatever grandpa God why the fuck does the boss keep you around this job I will never know".

"Probably to babysit little shit stains like yourself now shut the fuck up for a change and just leave me the hell alone ".

Tim didn't wait for a reply but he could here Martins mouth a running .

He paused to look back the noise of the chipper drown most of it but he could make out bits .

"You lazy old bastard " , "Your lucky I don't kick your ".

It was just then Martin threw a limb .
The damn thing had caught and caused him to lose his balance .
Tim ran but it was too late he was sucked into the chipper a spray of blood pine and bits of flesh was upon the wind as it blew all over hell and creation .

Tim hit the switch turned it off but nothing was left to save .

It was a true horror scene .

Martin always said one day he was out of here I bet he didn't think it would be in pieces .

And after the cops and all the bullshit that ensued Tim didn't look for the nearest bar he opted for home and a cold shower .
Martin had everything once but that silver spoon didn't mean shit when his ass was turned to pulp,

He drank that night away and sat out the following day.
He really had no desire to die for a dollar .
But least the job would be minus a short order prick whenever he did so choose to return .

Get It?

I hadn't written in days it used to be no matter the bender I could always deliver before the deadline.

Not anymore the train left the tracks but luckily in my case. I was still good enough most overlooked my bullshit.

A few had written me off.
But where one closed a door another was more than eager to overlook my bullshit for the quality of work.

I drank more and I wrote less.
A editor and friend rang my phone and for some reason I answered.

Simon was a punk kid when I first met him.
A goof ball with a drive who wanted to run a small press and was a fan of my work.

"Hey chief surprised you answered."

"Yeah surprised myself as well what can I do for you."

"Man I need some work from you, you got anything? I'm having a hard time finding content."

"I might have some shit sitting around but I tell you it's not worth a crap."

"I doubt that man your stuffs always solid."

I laughed.

"Yeah you been studying my stuff kid? You're a strange bird indeed but hey no need to stay in the closet these days."

"Shit I thought I was in the basement like some demented mad scientist."

"Or maybe just locked in a cage like some retarded child."

"Wow kinky I like it."

Simon was a nut but always good for a laugh.

I knew he was doomed as far as his press went but I would go through my backlog and find something.

We shot the shit for a while then said our goodbyes.
I sent him four writes then poured a drink and was done for the evening.

Sometimes you realize words are an escape as well as a prison and the more you become known for them you simply dig your own grave.

The press was dead in a year.
My work went on and soon I found more avenues that would fade as quickly as they got off the ground.

A hamster in a wheel just keeps running.
There's no point to this story .
Sorry no refunds today.

Cheers For The Bad Guy

I didn't enjoy the party I lived everyday like the
motherfucker was my last .

My two favorite girls bourbon and the page were always
never far from hand and seldom in control.

You want the best from anyone never shackle and you will
thrive in the chaos of a life lived uncertain .

A gas pedal down a wild one on top and no concern for the
safety we lived where others only choose to exist .

Indulge in every whim and leave behind a pleasant scar .

It's always in their eyes and the passion will pass you by
like a corvette down the expressway .

Leaving you behind with such an incredible view as she
chases another endless goodtime in the sunset .

Making the wolves howl and old dogs whimper .
Some just can simply shift the gears without even touching
the clutch .

The bad will always catch your eye and the worst leave
you with something far better .

They are the first to close the bar the last to hit the floor .

Castings shadows that remain standing tall like statues
leaving monuments to a good time in their wake .

We all burn out either way .

I Write For Myself

The words have always found a home even when I could
not say the same .

Memories now are like a cancer I cannot afford to keep
inside .
So I will simply move past what never served me any good
to begin with.

It used to be the road ahead was a supersize now it's more
a dead calm that reminds me it all has to end sometime.

I never planned anything for life was never certain .
The only thing I did was wait for whatever would be .

I didn't get much out of writing this .
And you probably thought much the same.

Secondhand Serenade

Love is a con and one of the worst kind a man cannot be prepared for.
The high ,The release , The orgasm a drug like any other .
I see people who view isolation a punishment .

I see people who never fully see themselves for the shallow pricks they truly are .

We all need a fix in some form or another .

Vice is a must for the adult masked simply as a child .

I need no reason to do as I please for I serve only myself with no remorse .

A old fool surrounded by many blind fools .
Don't sweat what others place upon you as a title .

I have no goal simply to drink fuck laugh and repeat .

Why do I have no clear direction ?
For no one told me of my true destination .

I hold no opinions of what I believe others should be.

The race is best ran never looking in the rearview .

Empty Bottles

In finding the bottle we slowly can lose something one drink at a time.

The bullshit that goes along with fear .
The friendships that change as quickly as the weather.

It's been one frozen ass winter I am overdue to know the warmth of the sun.

Everyone will turn on you eventually so never hang around long enough to become a nuisance .

I found the bottle it fit perfectly with the page .

Nothing else has remained such constant in my life .
Some call that the lack of one.

I never stayed long enough to hear them form an opinion such as this .

Don't waste a second of this life .

To Many A Hangover And One Night
Stand

Back when the bottle was fun and the miles were few .
I drifted in a bliss of fucked up soon to be fucked over .

She was by my side I still can't recall her name even
though I never forgot yours .

Morphine is great when you don't want to feel a thing and
you're in no true pain at all.

And sometimes in that fog when you finally come down it's
to find there's no longer anyone around .

I can't blame them but it never stopped me anyways .

The shit moments and the part time drama will make you
realize it beats nothing but not by much .

Watch that sunrise smoke what's left and wish the day
would never return.

I have no other excuse .
But give me some time I'm fresh out of a coma and new to
this reality shit.

This damn winter upon my soul just won't seem to end .
I really miss the feeling but I guess every addict does.

The strong always stand and the smart carry their ass
before the storm clears .

Cause everyone wants to party but nobody ever wants to be stuck cleaning up the mess.

When The Page Leaves The Writer

When the page leaves you it is far worse than any love
you may ever or will ever know.
For it is that which flows through our veins it is magic and
part of our souls all the same .

It has loved and left far better than yourself .
Papa knew it better than most ever truly will.
then one day it fled like the bird does before the storm .

He died broken taking the last thing he had in title only .
It drives the writer to madness much like the soldier who
no longer knows a battlefield yet still knows the sounds
and smells in his nightmares.

We all dream and yearn for that which has left us all the
same.
But only with the page can another not view your loss like
some limb torn from your body.

There is no scar or burn for others to sympathize .

And others whom still possess it will avoid you at all costs .
Fear shows the true nature of man .

Hold on to what you can before you lose it all the same .

I sat at the page for the last time .
Constructing what you are reading now.

This is not a last burst just simply the pages farewell.

Bricked In

You watched as I built the wall laying every brick with skill years of practice had taught me well.
A relationship is sacrifice of your sanity.

It is like driving head on into a tornado without a single regret .
Maybe it was the combined madness that took us so far and broke us all the same .

For you I cannot speak and as for me I no longer care to recall .

You stared in silence as the last few bricks were put in place .
We knew each other long enough to understand there just was no point in goodbyes .

And as I finished I realized it was I who was trapped within a prison of my own creation.
I needed an escape or at least a friend to bide the time.

Too bad you were not someone I could call that anymore .

I lit a smoke and admired my work .

It was solid it would be my reaper so to speak.
There was barely enough space to move let alone think.
It was a prison of my own creation it reminded me of our relationship pure hell in the worst way.

I did a great job .

I wondered if you would agree ?

Beer Over Butterflies

She said.

"can't we just go somewhere"?

I looked at her as we laid together in bed .
"Okay let's head to the bar"?

"I meant somewhere other than a bar can't we go to a park
or something"?

"Why the hell do you want to go to a park"?

"I just want to be outside breathe in air that isn't stale and
filled with smoke and the smell of old beer ".

She was younger than I and I could tell my world was far
too old for her .

She wanted to be amongst the trees feel the grass under
her feet and I rather not fight off ants and wasps in all that
is the bullshit of nature .

I would choose beer over butterfly's any day of the week.

There's One In Every Crowd

Never let fear get in the way of a good fight .

Maybe I lacked something from my childhood maybe I was far more a redneck than I ever care to let on .

But no more alive do you feel as in a fist fight .
It's never the loudmouth that boasts about his toughness you need to fear .

It's the man who sits silent in the corner drinking alone you need to avoid .
Most people simply like the sound of their own voice .
But the man in the corner wants to be left alone and nothing more .
Maybe he enjoys the chaos maybe he just had nowhere else to go.

The little man can never handle his shit and tries to make up for a lack in size with a boost of ego .
He flexes for all to see speaks as much as possible and tries to fuck everything in sight .

Then there are the ones who just enjoy a good fight .
The mad dog that can't imagine any other way to be .
He is a bully and blow hard but he packs a punch .

He picks out the weak and sets his eyes on the man who sits alone.

After enough of his shit the man in the corner beats the man down like a dog in the street.

He walks back in the bar and continues to drink .

The little man looks at him saying .

"Yeah your tuff but nothing compared to me ".

The man in the corner laughs to himself knowing there's always another fool ready to take a fallen one's place.

A Short Stories Reprise

When you find any sort of success your truly fucked in this life.

Frank thought to himself .
The last book finally was a hit a best seller his life was in shambles but he could finally afford his drinking and never seemed to lack for some company at the end of the night .

His bills were paid and he had no distractions to keep from the page .

Well besides himself .

The divorce was settled Susan had what she wanted the house and most the blood of his soul she moved on.
What a fucking big surprise that was .

It was no shock she already had one in the wings soon after his departure .

And here Frank was still living in a small motel on the Outer Banks.
But the bars were close the place suited his needs and he was happy with the view of the ocean right outside his door
.

Often he sat outside at night listening to the ocean not giving a damn about a single thing in this world.

He was a staple at the bars .
The page remained empty there just was less and less to say and more and more to drink and fuck with each and

every day.

Franks agent was the only reason he permanently left the phone off the hook.

Simon had a winning horse and he planned on riding this one all the way till the finish line or at least till he broke his leg and had to be put down .

Frank knew he had to call him eventually feed him the standard bullshit.

"The book is coming along fine kid no worries talk to me in July I should have it all dressed and ready for you to pick apart.

"Hey Frank just take it easy on the booze man I don't want you burning out before we even get started .

"Shit isn't that what all great writers do kid"?

"When I meet one I will tell you chief".

Simon was a prick but least he was a honest one .

That last conversation had been in February now summer approached and he hadn't written a single line .

Maybe the first novel was a total fluke now he would have to become a recluse to keep up interest but he knew that was a pipe dream he wasn't Salinger not even fucking close.

His life was a train wreck and every drink was one closer to oblivion.

He just couldn't stop and the sex was forgettable at best .
Susan was in his thoughts less and less now it was simply
an empty feeling that nothing seemed to touch .

Social drugs get replaced by the heavy shit and that
search to feel the bliss of feeling nothing at all.

The waves crashed into the shore and he drifted further
from thought the booze , the needle it all was far more
soothing than any story he could tell.

Eventually the party would end .

But by the time that day came Frank would be too wiped
slick to care taken like a bottle flung into the ocean now
swallowed up with the tide .

Empty pages are all he shall leave behind.

A Blank Page

For the first time I stared at the page and saw nothing but
emptiness .
No longer would the engine turn.
A sail without wind is simply left to wait .

A ornament and nothing more .
Maybe I had really done it this time.
Went on one to many bender .

I didn't know where it had went but it was gone .
And I was left to remain one of those sad burnouts .

Too fucked up to create too old to start something new.

Maybe I should just grab a gun and pull the trigger .
Erase the moment and create a morbid painting using my
brains splattered upon a wall that would be my canvas.

Maybe I just needed rest and a good meal.

Or maybe things were at the highways end .
Like some dog chasing its tail until it falls out in the floor
from exhaustion.

I didn't have an answer and I left the page just how I had
found it.
Blank and empty as myself .

I turned off the lights and locked it away from sight.

I dreamed of nothing that night.

Seems even in sleep something within my head was broken.

Where We Go Nobody Knows

He sat there his body worn out from living the fast life just a little too long.
They checked on him regular some made conversation.
Most just kept it basic nurse's had a job he didn't envy .

His liver was shot and his heart was weak he knew he wasn't leaving this place .

And to some degree he didn't give a damn .

He thought of old friends in the past .

Most all of them were in the ground .
And soon he would be joining them once again.

He didn't mind leaving this earth he just hated the thought of moving to a dry county in the sky.

He had to laugh to himself thinking back.

Cause upon further reflection he knew he damn sure wasn't going there .

And besides he wanted to see his friends again and they damn sure weren't going to be in Heaven either .

Cocktails With The Giant

They say Andre The Giant could easily drink over a
hundred beers .

Throw in a couple of bottles of wine and maybe a whiskey
or two you easily had a man whose record could never be
touched .

His tolerance is the Mount Everest of drinkers .

Nobody could match him no one dared to try .
He enjoyed a good laugh and was known to pass a huge
fart to amuse himself .

I believe Bukowski himself wouldn't try to top him .

He could hide a beer can in his hand so imagine what he
could do to your skull.

Hopefully if you ever drank with the Giant he picked up the
tab.

And if ever he passed out in the floor .

Well never wake a sleeping giant.
Let alone a hungover one named
Andre .

Status Report

I have drown myself in vices .
I have chased a good time till there is no time left.

The party has taken its toll on my body my mental status
has always been questionable at best.

I get wasted pass the fuck out find the page and chase
publication.
Others think I am lucky.

Those people are fools .
I bust my ass it is called work.

This job and yes it is a job.
It demands more than you can ever guess. .

It leaves you empty you become a robot not a person.

I can recite my bio with my eyes closed .
Other people say.

"Hey you really get around ".

I seldom reply .

It's not that I think I am better I just wanted this from day
one.

I imagined how it would be I was like anyone on the
outside looking in.

I didn't remotely have a fucking clue how it would be.

Sometimes I still don't have a clue I just wing it best I can.

My works got legs .
And I am a shell of my former self.

Payment in full blood and tears .

It is always work if you want to deal in luck .
Then fucking buy a lottery ticket !

No Readings Today

He hated giving readings .
Others always said .

But you have to do readings it's part of being a poet
everyone does readings .

Once made him wonder why?

With no other genre was there such a rule.

You didn't see Stephen King showing up at your door to
stand in the center of your cluttered living room to read
what you could so easily do yourself.

But all true poets do readings .
Another voice would say.

Once made him think.
Then maybe I am no true poet .

His words were strong and the page was full of life not
simply filled with words .

He didn't have a book out yet he had a long list of
publications .
Everyone said he was really coming up quick.

But he never gave a reading .

And this angered many.

He went to one once .
The top poets there were loud they acted up.

It wasn't about the page .
It was all about the show.
He remembered when he found the page himself .

It was order amongst the chaos.
He loved silence .

He was happy with the page .

He never gave a reading and this made most assume
things about him that were untrue .

He never gave a damn to perform for the crowd .
He was a writer not an actor after all.

Either way he would be forgotten just like all the rest.

The page is always there .

It waits and he creates.
Readings just weren't part of his job description .

Something Stinks

I live in a small ten by ten box most would refer to as a shed .
It's all I need and nothing more .

Outside there is a screen house I built when my life was spent with another .

She no longer breathes my air and I no longer taste her depression.

We were a disease that lay dormant for years .
Living as strangers acting instead of loving our time.

There's an old dog who has remained my companion .
He doesn't worry over tomorrow he just cares if his food will be served today.

People are far more fucked up than animals .

For only in false happiness do we as people exist .

My old dog just took a huge shit in the neighbor's yard .

Now we are both happy .

Sometimes old dogs can learn new tricks .

Too bad old poets can't find happiness in less worn out lines.

Boozer looks at me waiting for a bone he farts then walks away .

It's a hell of a stink .

Caring is not always sharing .

Through The Windows Pane

I am just a windows view to an empty room.
Where we can only imagine the story that once I called a life.

I don't know I can promise tomorrow when I am lucky just to make it through the day.

I just know the fantasy I once knew has left me in shambles
As empty as this room in which I stay.

If walls could speak I believe they would probably prefer to cry .

We all are empty tonight .

I wonder do you know I still remain behind this glass.

A reflected fool of this windows pain.

Random And Thoughtless

The thought of being normal truly frightens me.
Normal were the children I went to school with they thought
as they were told .

There paths were set for them.
I never cared for any true direction I lived for the moment
and my teachers tried to break me as so many others do
now.

I cared little for them I care even less for myself .
Words were my escape I clung to those of others till
learning to craft words of my own .

I knew the fist far easier than a warm embrace I hated
people .

Very little I have seen from humanity has led me to change
my opinion .

Normal is something to avoid at all cost .

Normal men kill for fun .
Normal women love like a light switch turning their
emotions off in a second .

The normal people replace what is not broken and cast a
downward view upon the man whom has less yet seems
happier than themselves .

I hide from these twisted fucks.
In fear one day I will awake to find myself amongst them.

Keep my life in steady time as a drummer in a marching band .
Going to the state fair with the kids in some small town .

We all see it differently I suppose.

But however we find our happiness I believe lost within the freak show I shall remain .

Kids

I read yet another had taken a fall.
Saw no further path so he simply ended it all the same .

He was young but death doesn't discriminate .
His face was that of someone whom could chase dreams
or at least a hot piece of ass .

I envied his balls .
For to take your own life meant fear was never your issue .

Kids are often fearless and fools all rolled together in a
promising package .

But least they weren't running from a ending they could not
avoid .

I never thought a person was weak for checking out early .
But I didn't romanticize it either .

To swing from a rope or bite the bullet still left for a terrible
scene and probably a load of shit in your pants .

I believe I rather do as an animal and silently vanish into
the night.
To decay maybe in the woods and hopefully never be
found .

I commit suicide slowly with the bottle and a bleeding ulcer
wrapped together in an it's all in a good time disguise .

Sometimes its painful most times there's no longer a buzz
involved.

And last night there was forgettable company to share the
moments I would not recall.

She was fractured as well .
We were alive for now .
But eventually we would all die .

I thought of the kid for a second after she was gone.
I believe his company would have been far better looking..

But then again so probably would have been mine if I
hadn't stayed around so long.

I swallowed a few pills and slept till the afternoon.

I would of checked out then but I forgot to leave a note .
I may be self-destructive but still I believed in manners .

Love Like A Storm

Before the rain as the winds kick up and others run like chickens with their heads cut off .

Seeking shelter fearing the wrath of nature I usually prefer to have a seat mix a drink and welcome the chaos.

The best storms are like jilted lovers fiery in nature and void of concern.

The smell of the earth before the rain a perfection none can describe and I embrace her nature and understand it will destroy you eventually .

A true work of art is always dangerous and seldom in control.

The storm is a truth we must understand and far too many ignore .

I have rode out many upon these waters as far too many men have before me .

Like an old sea captain or pirate I am but at her mercy .

If I fall tonight then I go out happy.

There's always something perfectly tragic like love and an oncoming storm.

Please Do Not Disturb

Philip got used to no peace in his life but there was never any getting used to Sully .

He sat there in his recliner pissed off he didn't even know what the fuck to say let alone how to start off the conversation.

"Dude I'm telling you it's no big deal Veronica will get over it ,what you think it's the first dick she ever saw "?

"Jesus Christ Sully you can't just jerk off whenever or wherever you want this is my fucking house "!

"Dude I didn't know you were bringing her home what you think I want an audience when I jerk off you sick fucker".

Sully was a weird bird a unemployed want to be standup comedian and one funny bastard in small doses .

Phil took him in when he fell down on his luck it was only supposed to be for a little while .
That was three years ago.

He had a blast with Sully but like anything after the party ended the real shit was too much .

Sully drank nonstop kept late hours came home sometimes with company yeah comics were funny but off the stage they were a mixed bag of assorted pricks and miserable bastards.

Last night was the final straw .
Phil had been after Veronica for a while and finally last night was the moment .

The mood was set then he walks through the door with Veronica to find Sully on his couch dick in hand some weird ass porn on the TV.

Needless to say Veronica was not staying the night .

"Sully the shit has to end man I can't even bring women back here because of you ".

Sully as always laughed as he laid back on the couch it seemed like the fucker was glued to it as much time as he spent there lately.

"Dude lighten up , Like you don't masturbate duh who doesn't jerk off"?

"Not in the fucking living room I gave you a room I don't charge you rent can't you at least do that shit in your own fucking room"?

" The fucking big screen is out here you prick and you know I don't have a TV ".

"Well I'm sorry I didn't provide you with a TV to watch porn on Sully fuck man do you ever visit are planet from time to time"?

"Man you think Veronica was turned on by me stroking my

156

dick and that's why she left , I mean she had that weird look in her eyes ".

"Cause she walked in to a guy jacking off on my couch you fucking nut "!

The argument was pointless Sully turned everything into a joke .
And funny as he was it got old quick.

"Man you're really uptight dude I'm just saying want me to put on some porn really takes the edge off".

He busted up laughing once it wasn't unusual for Sully to laugh at his own jokes cause if he didn't nobody usually would.

"Fuck you Sully ".

Phil said finally laughing once was always a mistake with a joker because they were just like bad children .

Once you gave them attention they seldom calmed down.

"Man I am sorry I ruined your action last night but seriously dude I mean I kinda felt that three way vibe in the air ".

"Yes of course what woman wouldn't look at your three inch cock and not get instantly wet right".

Sully laughed .

"Hey I knew you fucking looked dude I would have shown you long before that I mean you're like my brother ".

"Why in the fuck would I want to see your dick"?

"Beats the hell out of me you sick bastard but I'm telling you I think Veronica was down for a three way ".

"Your fucking nuts you know that"?

Sully cracked a beer once was part of his usual morning routine.

"What are you worried when you're at one end and I'm at the other you will look deep in my eyes and have a moment or something "?

"You are so sick it's not even funny ".

Sully laughed and flipped on the TV and cut a fart .

"I'm telling you bud we can just cut out the middle man I mean woman dude why suppress yourself "?

"Man just shut the fuck up and pass me a beer you cheap prick".

Sully tossed him a tallboy from the four pack he had on the floor .

"That's the spirit Philly , man you were pissed off last night ".

"Who said I'm still not "?

"Hell man I am sorry wasn't like I planned it, You call her

up "?

I didn't reply .
And eventually we just stopped talking .

Sully was a perfect storm of a good time and natural
disaster all rolled into one .

We watched TV and eventually had to go grab some more
beers .

He was funny enough to be making his living at making
people laugh .

Most called him a bum I just called him my brother .
Whenever I came home unexpectedly I always learned to
knock first .

Veronica never did talk to me again .
And Sully never did shut the fuck up about it .

Some people never step down from the stage .
The laugh should never linger .

Sully eventually moved away
I haven't had a good laugh in months .

I heard someone spotted Veronica with Sully at one of his
shows they were all over one another .

Sully never once thanked me for introducing them.

Guess the jokes on me .

Booze

Dear Bottle

We have spent so many great years together .
Most I can't recall but those people some refer to as
friends told me I had a blast .

You were there when I met my future ex-wife .

She was always jealous of you .
I cannot imagine why.
We kissed but it was nothing more .

She screwed half her coworkers yet was never named
employee of the month seems kind of pointless to me .

You killed my liver but I still love you so.

We have a truly abusive relationship but least you haven't
given up on me yet.

I would put a ring on you if only you had a hand .
I'm always great with excuses .

Maybe that's why I never quit drinking from your well my
dear.

Every beautiful woman needs a love letter.

And this one's for you .
My ever eternal passion .

No one can ever say I lack dedication .

My dearest .

Booze .

Fuck The World

She said.
"It's all gone to shit"
As she walked into the living room.

"The world ?, I believe that went to shit a long time
ago sweetheart."
I replied to her not even looking up from my paper .

"No!"
Angel replied.

"Not the world ,Fuck the world the nets out."

It was then I knew this relationship was strictly sexual.

John Patrick Robbins

Cover art by Red Focks and Ammi Romero

ALSO AVAILABLE FROM ALIEN BUDDHA PRESS

Mar-a-Lago Teetotaler by Maxwell Ryder

The Art of Changing Nothing to Punk Gigs by Sudeep Adhikari

Vegas Poems by Ryan Quinn Flanagan

Frenetic/No Contest by Dustin Pickering

Winds of Time by JoyAnne O'Donnell

Alien Buddha Cums to Jesus by Jay Miner and Jeff Flipski

Dimensional High by Ammi Romero

Poison in Paradise by Scott Thomas Outlar

LOCOmotion of Life by Adam Levon Brown

Screamo Lullabies by Robert J.W

Surfing the Appalachian Vortex by Mark Hartenbach

Irritable Brain Syndrome by Willie Smith

About Consciousness by Heath Brougher

Heroin by Catfish McDaris

36 Haikus and a Horror Story by Red Focks

Vanilla, Lemon, Blood by Ron Androla

Icarus Rising by Don Beukes

Flakka by Ryan Quinn Flanagan

Our Little Hope by Bree

Bartholomew: The Rapture by Ammi Romero

The Past is Calling by Thasia Anne

Witness Protection Program by Mark Hartenbach
and Red Focks

Death to Fairy Tales by Alex S. Johnson

Deathbed Colored Glasses by Rob Plath

A Stab in the Dark by Bengt O Björklund

Adventures in Space and Other Selected Casualties
by Richard D. Houff

Words Whispered and Screamed Over the Great
Lakes by Jeremy Stolz

Duffy Street & Other Dubious Incidents by Red
Focks

Death is Not Our Holy Word by Adam Levon
Brown

A Ludicrous Split by Kevin Ridgeway and Gabriel Ricard

Little Hollywood by Luke Kuzmish

It's Colder Than Hell/ Starving Elves Eat Reindeer Meat/ Santa Claus is Dead by Jeff Weddle

The Diablo's Pistolas by Stefan Bohdan

God's Silence a Lion's Roar by Stefan Bohdan

This Useless Beauty by Jason Baldinger

Home Memories by Gideon Cecil

Return to Vegas Poems by Ryan Quinn Flanagan

Dusty Video Game Cartridges by Robert J.W.

Somebody's Book of the Dead by Mark Borczon

Zugzwang by R. Keith

Poetry Is: A Dirty Word by Richard J Cronborg

The House by Heidi Blakeslee

Belly Laughs by Chelsea Bergeron

No One Approves Of My Methods by Clinton J.
Ruttan

The Black and the Blues by Jay Passer

Mannequin Legs & Other Tales by Robert Ragan

Philosopher's Ship by John Grochalski

Crashing the Zen Piñata by Mark Hartenbach

Howl Drunkenly at the Moon by Nathan Tompkins

Freud's Haberdashery Habit by Mike Fiorito

(Pseudonym Lastname #1) Anime Fight Battle:
Japan by Red Focks and Ammi

Cave Dreams to Star Portals by Chani Zwibel

In Which The World is Turned Upside Down: & an
idiot is running the country by Thomas R. Thomas

Sideways Blues by Carl Kaucher

Hungry Words by R. Bremner

Made in the USA
Middletown, DE
30 December 2018